Usborne Activi...

Over 50 Brain Games

Written by
Lucy Beckett-Bowman

Illustrated by Non Figg and Molly Sage

Are the sides of these squares bending?

1 Spot the difference

Study this scene, then compare it with the one on the right.

Circle **ten** differences in this scene.

Grid lines

1. There are nine squares in the grid below. Can you write the numbers 1 to 9 in the grid, so that each horizontal, vertical and diagonal line adds up to 15? Two numbers have been filled in for you.

2. Can you place six Xs in the grid below without making three-in-a-row in any direction?

Magic bean

Rob's dad gave him a magic bean for his birthday. He promised him that the bean would grow into a huge plant very quickly.

That Tuesday night, Rob planted the bean in a flowerpot and put it on the windowsill in his bedroom. When Rob checked the bean the next morning, he could see a little green shoot poking out of the soil.

The following morning, the shoot had exactly doubled in size, and each morning after that he found that the plant had doubled in size again.

By Friday of the following week, the plant completely filled his room!

On which day did the magic plant half-fill Rob's room?

Answer:

Arctic argument

Four greedy polar bears can't learn to share their fishing holes. The only way to settle the argument is to divide the ice into four pieces, each with its own fishing hole. Each piece must have 16 squares, and they must all be the same shape. One piece has been drawn for you – can you draw the others?

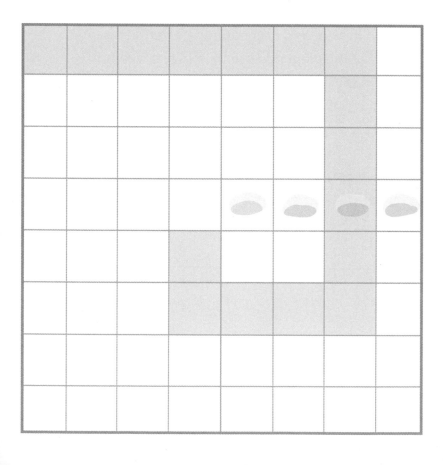

The magic number

Think of any number you like.
Write it in the next column:

Multiply this number by 2:

Add 12 to the answer:

Then take away 3:

Now add 5:

Divide by 2:

Take away the original number:
What did you get?

Now try again, starting with a different
number. What do you notice?

Non-stop draw

Can you draw along all the lines in these pictures without going over any line more than once, or taking your pencil off the page?

A

B

Making squares

1. Can you change the number of squares from five to seven by **moving** just **two** lines? You can't leave any unconnected lines.

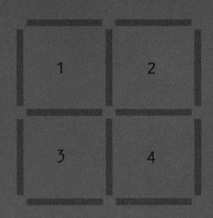

(Square 5 is the outer square.)

Try the puzzle here:

2. Can you make these six squares into three squares by **taking away three** of the lines? You can't leave any unconnected lines.

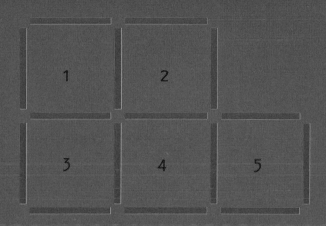

(Square 6 is the outer square around 1-4.)

Try the puzzle here:

Hexagon halves

Cutting the red hexagon in half, as shown below, makes two pieces that are exactly the same shape.

Some of the shapes on the right can be made by two smaller pieces that are the same shape as the hexagon halves, and some of them can't.

Draw circles around the shapes that **can't** be made by two pieces like the ones shown below.

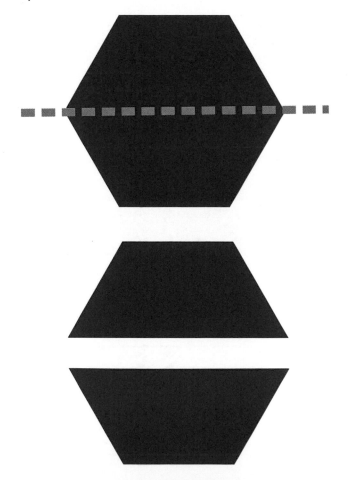

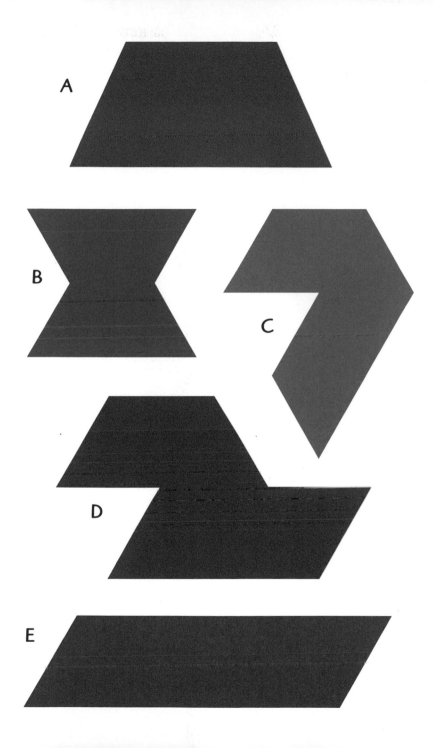

A

B

C

D

E

Toy blocks

1. Ellie has been playing with Joe's toy blocks, even though he asked her not to. Joe always stacks them in a specific order, and Ellie needs to put them back where they were, so he won't know she's touched them. All she remembers is that:

• The orange was either at the top or the bottom.

• The strawberries block was the fifth one down.

• The blue flower was in between the pear and the apple.

• The banana was directly above the pear.

Write the numbers 1 to 7 next to the blocks to help Ellie put them back in the correct order, using 1 for the top block.

2. There are five toy blocks below. How many different ways can you arrange the blocks in a line, if the kite block is always at the top, and the cloud block is always at the bottom?

Answer:

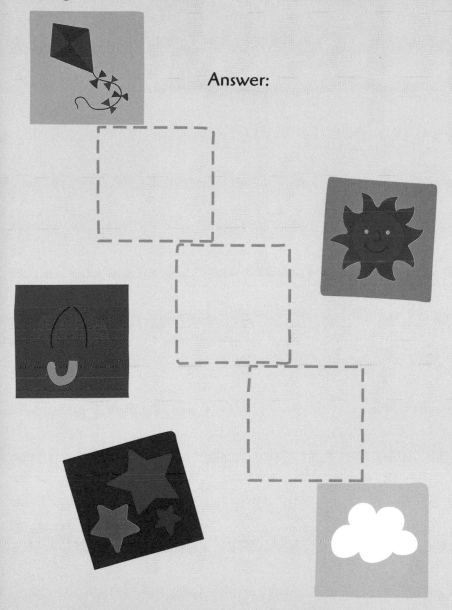

Riddles

1. Alex lives on the twelfth floor in a tall building. Every day when he leaves his home, he presses the button in the elevator that takes him to street level. When he comes home at the end of the day, he pushes the button that takes him to the tenth floor, and walks the last two flights of stairs. Why does he do this?

2. A black cat is sleeping in the middle of a black road. There are no streetlights and there's no moonlight. A car comes speeding down the road with its lights off and its stereo blasting. As it gets close to the cat, it slows down and safely steers around it. How did the driver know the cat was there?

3. Nikki was walking her dog through some fields on a bright, sunny morning when she came across an old hat and scarf and some lumps of coal lying on the ground. Why were they there?

4. A man lives in an orange bungalow. Inside there is an orange cat, an orange fish, an orange chair, an orange table – everything is orange, except the stairs. Why?

Broken clock

Andrew's alarm clock loses ten minutes every hour.
Exactly one hour ago, it stopped working completely,
showing the time as 8:50. Andrew knows he set it to
the correct time at 6:20. What time is it now?
Draw your answer on the clock below.

You can use these old clocks to help work out your answer.

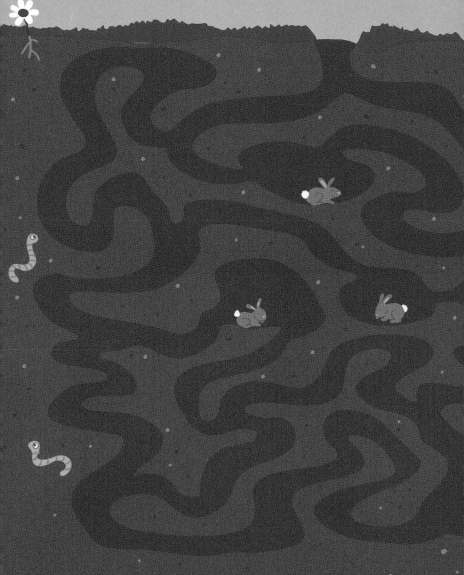

Rabbit warren

Seven baby rabbits are waiting for their food. Can you draw a route for the mother rabbit to follow that takes her past all the baby rabbits? She cannot use any part of a tunnel more than once.

Word ladders

Can you turn the word at the top of each ladder into the word at the bottom? Fill in the spaces on the ladders with a new word, changing one letter at a time.

For example:

BUG

··· ··· ···

BEE

HAND

··· ··· ··· ···

B ··· ··· ···

F ··· ··· ···

··· ··· ··· ···

FOOT

PAW

··· ··· ···

JAM

BEAR

··· ··· ··· ···

··· ··· ··· T

··· ··· ··· ···

BULL

TEA

··· ··· ···

··· ··· ···

POT

WING

··· ··· ··· ···

··· ··· ··· ···

BIRD

HEAT

··· ··· ··· ···

··· ··· ··· ···

··· ··· ··· ···

COLD

Crazy cubes

1. Some of these shapes will fold up to make a cube, and some of them won't. Draw a circle around each one you think **will** fold up to make a cube.

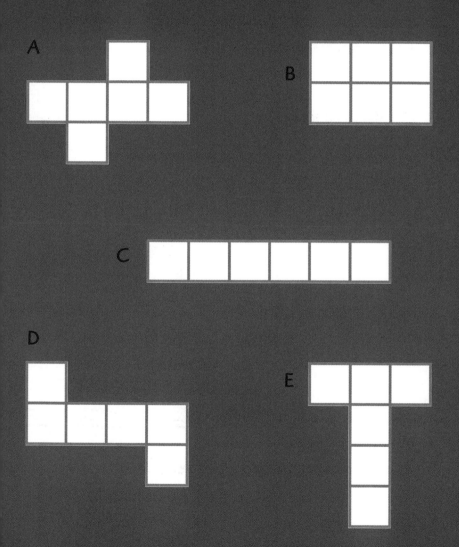

2. This large cube is made up of 64 little ones. If you paint all over the outside of the big cube, and then break it up into all the little cubes, can you work out how many of the little cubes **will not** have paint on them?

Answer:

Splitting circles

1. Can you divide this circle into **seven** sections, using just **three** straight lines?

2. Using **three** straight lines that go from edge to edge, can you divide this circle into **five** sections, so that the numbers in each section all add up to the same amount?

The two mice

When Dobbin the donkey arrived at the farm, he was rather annoyed to find two mice blocking his way into the stables. Each mouse was guarding a different door.

"Get out of my way!" Dobbin said to the mice.

"You're only allowed to go through one of the doors," said Percy the pig, who was passing by. "Behind one door is a bucket full of juicy carrots and a trough of cool water. There's nothing to eat or drink at all behind the other door."

"But how do I know which door leads to the carrots and water?" asked Dobbin.

"Just ask one of the mice," Percy answered. "But you can only ask one mouse one question. One mouse always lies, and the other always tells the truth."

Dobbin thought hard, but he didn't know what to do. Do you know what question Dobbin should ask one of the mice to help him choose the right door?

Answer:

Cog rotation

1. A professor has finally completed a crazy egg-smashing machine. The problem is, he can't remember which way to turn the machine's handle to make it break the eggs. Can you help him?

2. Draw circles around the two groups of cogs that match each other exactly when one is turned over and rotated.

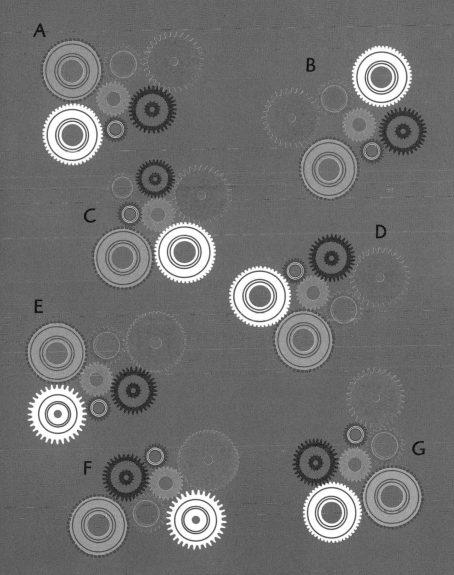

Puzzling patterns

1. Each of the rows below follows the same pattern, leading on to the next row. Can you find the pattern and draw the last step in the space at the end?

A

B

C

2. The four boxes below follow a pattern. See if you can spot the pattern, then fill in the blank box.

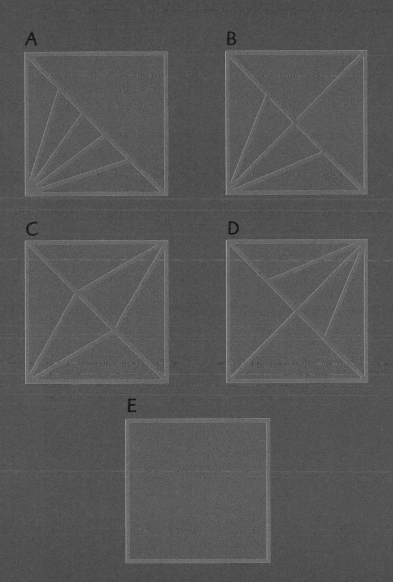

A

B

C

D

E

Searching for shapes

1. How many rectangles can you count here, including the ones made when they overlap? Be careful – there are more than you might think.

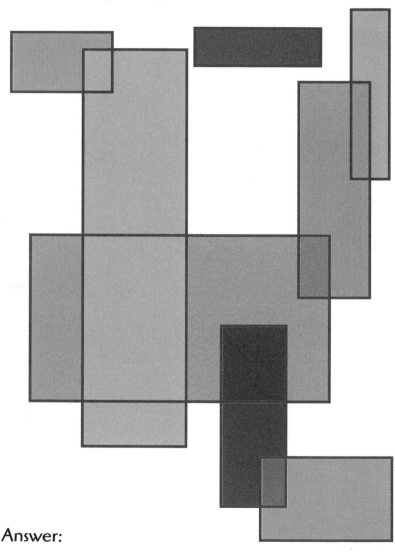

Answer:

2. When you first look at the picture below, it's easy to count 16 squares – but there are a lot more than that! Can you find them all? Use a pencil to help you figure out how many squares there are, then write the answer below.

Answer:

The cat in the well

Tabby the cat was feeling very curious one day, and decided to jump down a well to see what was at the bottom. Unfortunately, she didn't find anything interesting down there – and didn't have a plan for how to get out again!

The wall of the well was made of large red bricks, and was 20 bricks high. Tabby dug her claws into the cracks between the bricks and pulled herself up by five bricks every day. This was very tiring for Tabby, and every night she'd slide back down four bricks. How many days did it take Tabby to reach the top of the well?

Answer:

Counting cakes

The scales in the pictures below are all evenly balanced. However, the last set of scales is missing its cupcakes. Can you figure out how many cupcakes are needed to balance the scales? Draw them on.

Optical illusions

Look closely at these pictures, then answer the questions. The answers may not be quite what you expect...

1. Which of these lines is longer, A or B?

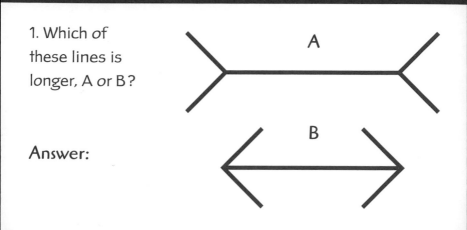

Answer:

2. Which line follows the same path as the white line – red, blue, yellow or green?

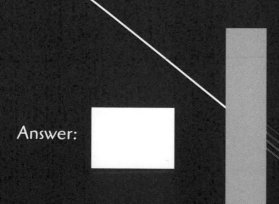

Answer:

3. Which of
the middle
circles is
bigger, A
or B?

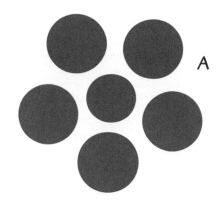

A

Answer:

B

4. In which of these
pictures are the four
balls further up the
background, A or B?

A

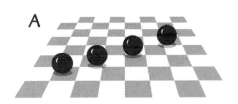

B

Answer:

Flowerpots

Can you place ten flowerpots in the garden below, so that they are arranged in five lines, with four pots in each line? The lines can go vertically, horizontally or diagonally, and will make up a familiar shape – the flowerpots below may give you a clue...

Spot the difference

Study this scene, then compare it with the one on the right.

Circle **ten** differences in this scene.

Dominoes

1. Each row of dominoes follows a pattern. See if you can spot the pattern in each row, then fill in the missing dots on the blank dominoes.

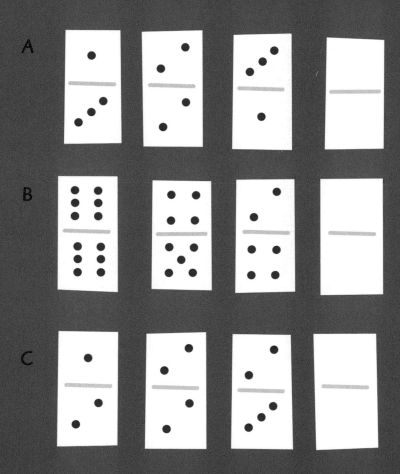

2. The loose dominoes are missing from the chain. Work out where they should go, then add the spots in the right places. Be careful – one of the pieces is a double-blank.

Troll toll

Jake's best friend, Marie, lives on the other side of the valley. On his way to see her, Jake has to go past seven greedy, chocolate-eating trolls.

Each troll guards one of the seven bridges that Jake needs to cross to reach Marie's house. The trolls won't let him cross unless he pays a fee, or toll – in chocolate. Jake has to give each troll half of the number of chocolate bars he is carrying. However, even though the trolls are greedy chocolate-eaters, they aren't mean (or very clever), so each troll always gives back one bar.

Jake has figured out exactly how many bars he needs to take with him to be able to pay the seven troll tolls, and have two bars left over – one for himself and one for Marie. Do you know how many bars he must take?

Answer:

Pyramid puzzles

1. In this pyramid, each number is the sum of the two directly underneath it. Write the missing numbers on the blank blocks.

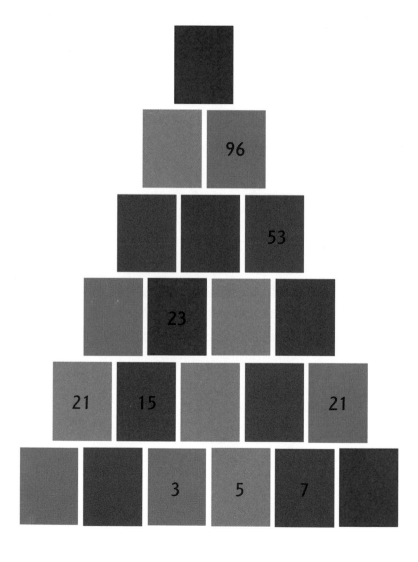

2. Which number should be placed in the middle of the last pyramid?

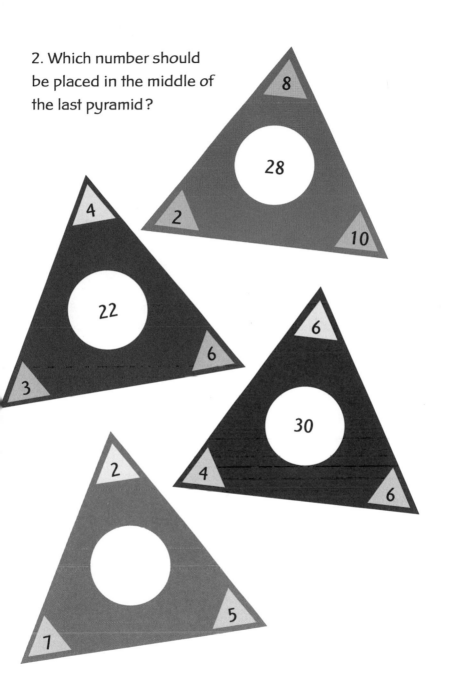

See-saws

In each set of three see-saws, a triangle, a square and a circle each weigh a different amount. The first two see-saws in each set are perfectly balanced, but the last one is missing one shape on the **right-hand side**. For each set, draw the shape that will make the last see-saw balance.

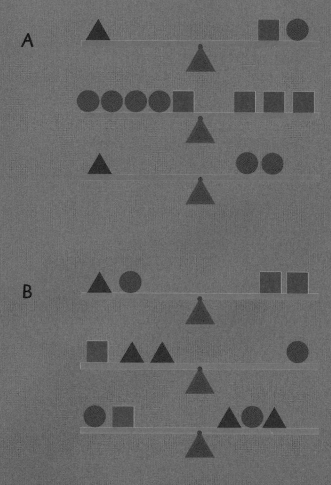

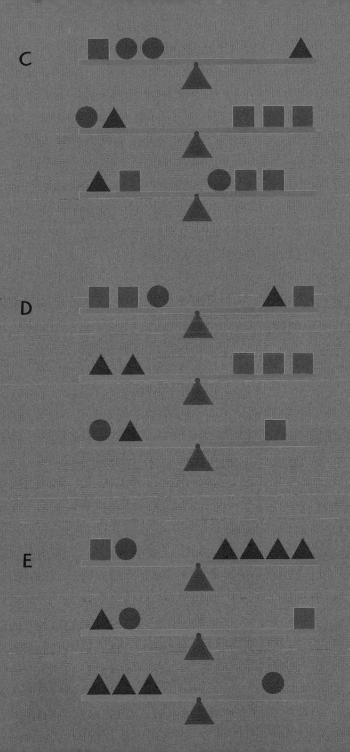

Shearing sheep

The nine sheep below need to be put into separate pens so the farmer can shear them. Can you put each sheep in its own pen by drawing just **three** squares around them? No curved lines are allowed.

Strange shapes

Some of the shapes below are very unusual. They can be drawn on paper, but they cannot actually exist in real life – they are impossible shapes. Can you figure out which of the shapes are possible, and which are impossible? Write 'P' for possible, or 'I' for impossible, next to each shape.

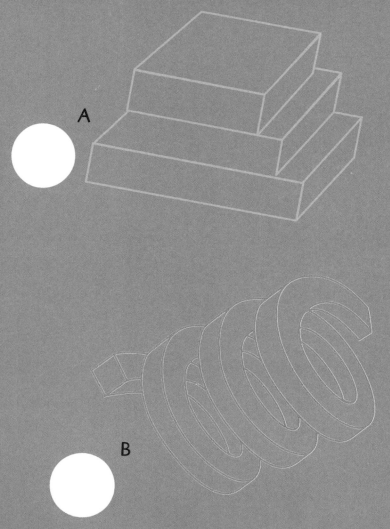

A

B

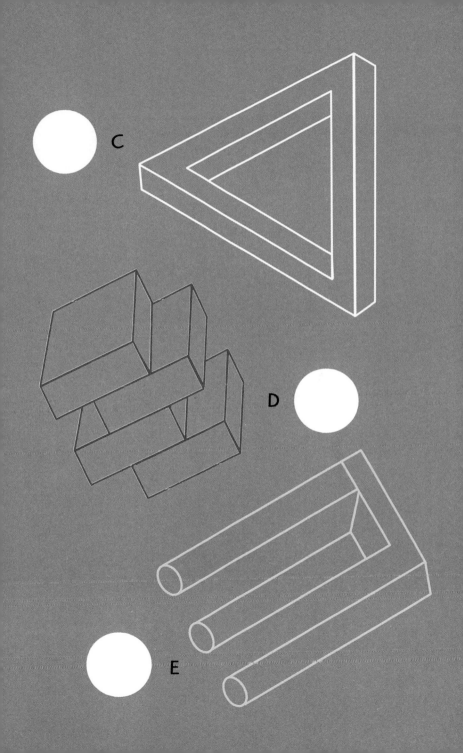

C

D

E

Cutting hair

Emma went to visit her aunt, who lived on a very small island. One day, Emma wanted to get her hair cut. Her aunt told her that there were only two hairdressers on the whole island, so Emma decided to visit both before choosing where to go.

She looked in the window of the first hairdresser's shop, and saw that the place was filthy. The hairdresser's own hair was very uneven and was badly dyed.

The second hairdresser's shop was clean and tidy, and Emma noticed that the hairdresser had very nice hair.

After seeing this, she went straight back to the first hairdresser's shop and got her hair cut there.

Why would she do this?

Answer:

Spiders and flies

1. Avoiding the trapped flies, can you guide the spider to the middle of its web? The letters you pass through on the way should spell out a word. Write it at the bottom of the page.

Answer:

2. Every hungry spider needs a fly to eat. Using only **two** straight lines, can you divide the web below into **three** areas, with two spiders and two flies in each one?

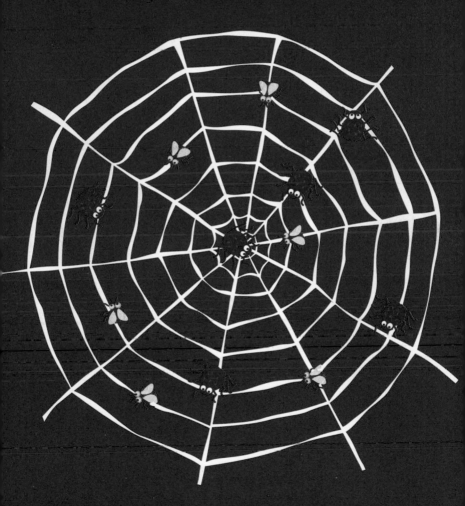

Telling time

Each column of clock faces on the right follows a different pattern. Can you see what the patterns are, then fill in the hour and minute hands on the blank clock faces?

So many triangles

How many triangles can you find in these three shapes? Draw over the lines in the shapes to help you spot the triangles. There are more than you might think, so look carefully.

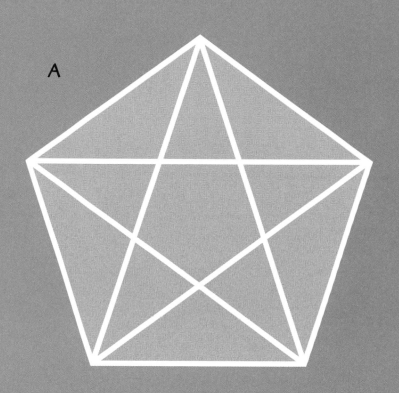

A

Answer:

B

Answer:

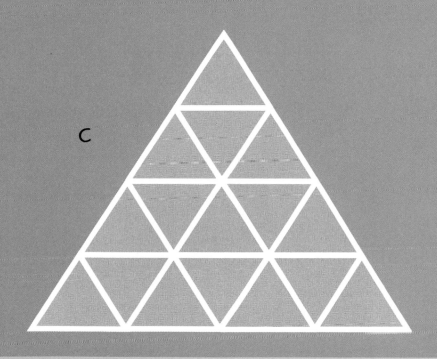

C

Answer:

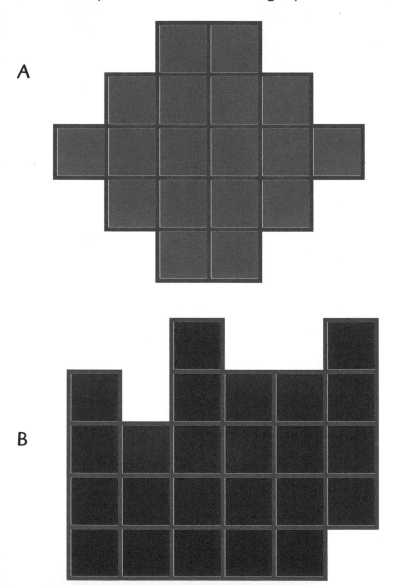

Shape splitting

Draw along the lines between the squares to divide each of the shapes below into **six** identical pieces that are made up of whole squares. There can't be any squares left over.

A

B

C

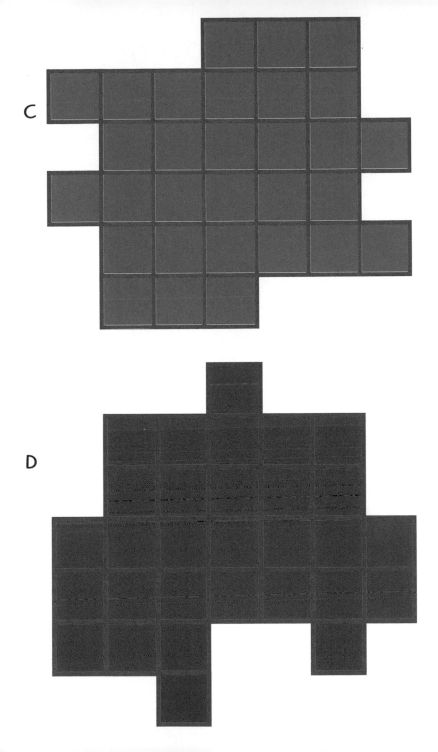

D

Alphabet puzzles

1. Some letters of the alphabet are missing from the bubbles below. Work out which letters are missing, then rearrange those letters to find out what's making all the bubbles!

Answer:

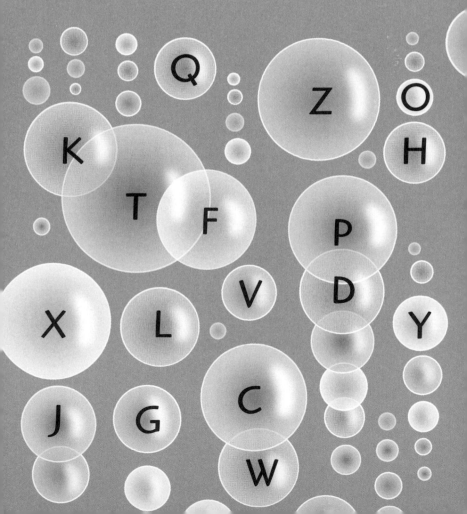

2. What's special about the following sentence?
'The quick brown fox jumps over the lazy dog.'

Answer:

3. All the letters of the alphabet have been split into
the two groups below. What's different about the two
groups of letters? Write your answer underneath.

A E F H I K
L M N T V
W X Y Z

B C D
G J O P
Q R S U

Answer:

Magician's cups

Mungo the Magician always starts his act with a challenge for the audience. He places ten cups upside down in the shape of a triangle, then asks, "Can anyone move just **three** of the cups, so that the triangle is pointing down instead of up?"

Try your hand at Mungo's challenge. In the triangle below, circle the three cups you would move, and draw arrows to show where you would put them.

River crossing

You are standing on one side of a river with a cat, a mouse, and a big piece of cheese. You need to take the cat, mouse and cheese across to the other side of the river, but you can only take over one thing at a time.

• If you leave the cat and the mouse alone together, the cat will eat the mouse.

• If you leave the mouse and the cheese alone together, the mouse will eat the cheese.

How can you take the cat, mouse and cheese across the river in the fewest number of crossings?

Answer:

Bricks and bees

1. You have three pairs of bricks – one pair is red, one pair is green and one pair is blue. The bricks in each pair weigh the same as each other, and all six bricks are the same size. One pair of bricks is heavier than the others. You have some balancing scales to weigh the bricks, but you're only allowed to use them once. How can you find out which pair of bricks is the heaviest?

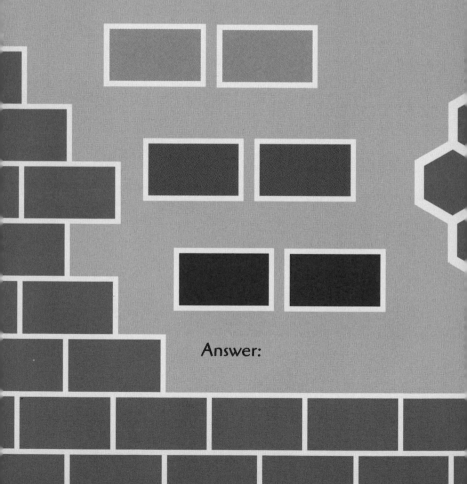

Answer:

2. Can you fill in the missing numbers in the two orange hexagons? Think about the direction you move in to get to the next hexagon.

Tricky questions

Can you answer these tricky questions? The answers might not be quite what you expect.

1. 'This senttence has three misteaks in it.'
Can you see what they are?

Answer:

2. A greedy girl bought ten cream cakes and ate all but four. How many did she have left to share with her friend?

Answer:

3. How many times can you take away 9 from 39?

Answer:

4. If two people can dig two holes in two days, how long does it take one person to dig one hole?

Answer:

5. If yesterday's tomorrow was Thursday, what day is tomorrow's yesterday?

Answer:

6. You have a bag full of six oranges. How can you give an orange each to six people, and still have one left in the bag?

Answer:

Fencing goats

1. Three grumpy goats need to be put in separate pens to stop them from fighting. Use a pencil to draw **seven** fences around the goats, making sure that the fences don't cross each other. Use the fence post at the side as a guide for the length of each fence, but don't include it as part of your answer.

2. Draw lines to divide the grid into **six** areas. Each area must contain the same number of squares as goats. One area has been done for you.

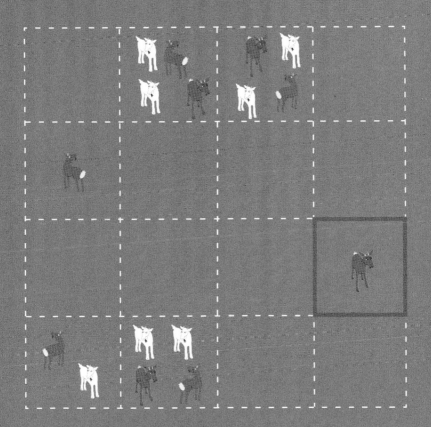

Star systems

1. The aim of this puzzle is to draw stars in the grid below, but there are rules about where stars can and can't be placed:

• Every striped square must have **one** star next to it, either horizontally or vertically.
• Stars cannot be placed next to each other vertically, horizontally or diagonally.
• The numbers next to the grid show how many stars must be in that row or column.

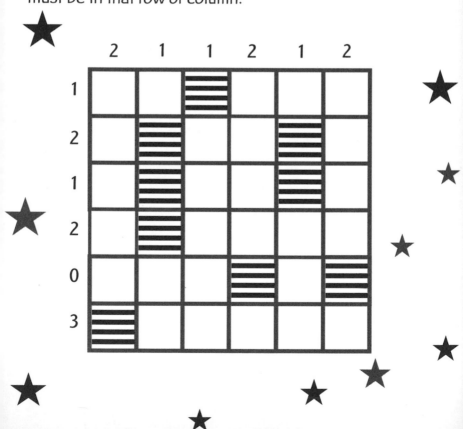

2. The grid below is made up of six blocks, each made up of six squares. Fill in the blank squares, so that every row, column and block contains all six symbols shown on the right.

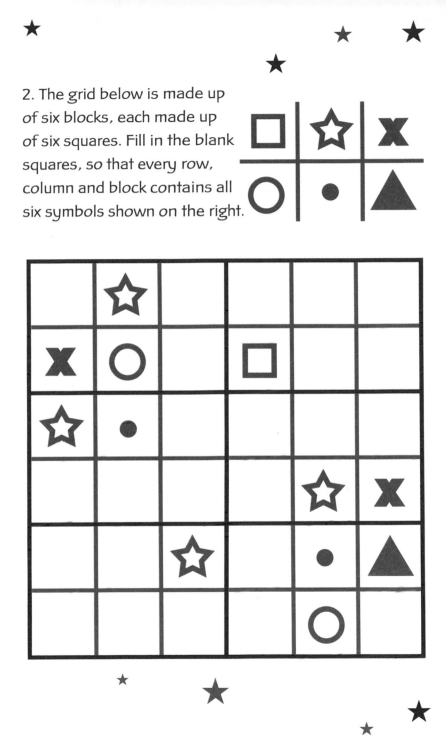

Joining dots

1. In the grid below, you can make lots of squares by joining four dots with straight lines. How many squares is it possible to make? (Don't forget that you can draw diagonal lines, too.)

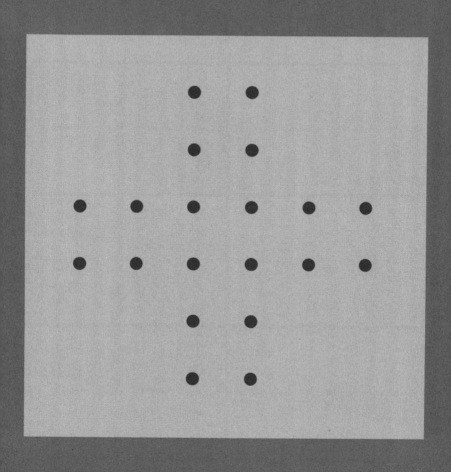

Answer:

2. Using just **four** straight lines, can you join all of the dots in the grid below, without taking your pencil off the page?

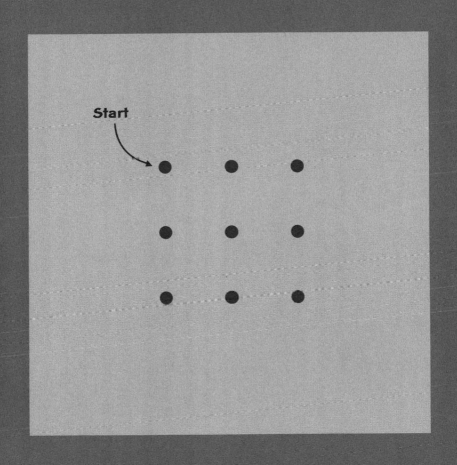

Start

Crossing the bridge

Ellie, Josh, Isaac and Mia need to cross a rickety old bridge to get home. It's dark, and no one wants to cross the bridge without the lantern – but it's only safe for two people to cross at a time.

Each person walks at a different speed:
Ellie can cross the bridge in one minute.
Josh can cross the bridge in two minutes.
Isaac can cross the bridge in five minutes.
Mia can cross the bridge in ten minutes.

They only have 17 minutes to get to the other side,
or they'll be late home. How can they do this?

Use this space for any workings out to help you
solve the puzzle.

Butterfly twins

Two of these butterflies are identical twins. Find which ones they are, and draw circles around them.

Points of view

The trays A, B, C and D all look like the tray below, shown from different angles. However, only one of the trays has the shapes inside arranged in exactly the same way. Draw a circle around the one that matches.

A

B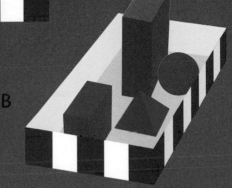

C

D

Letters apart

1. The aim of this puzzle is to write the first eight letters of the alphabet (A, B, C, D, E, F, G and H) in the boxes below. Can you fill in the boxes, so that none of the letters that are next to each other in the alphabet are in boxes that are touching either horizontally, vertically or diagonally?

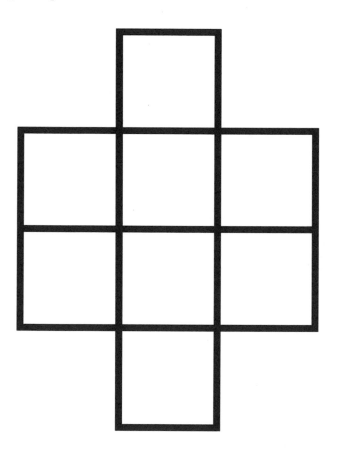

2. Can you find a nine-letter word to do with mazes hiding in the grid below? Move horizontally, vertically or diagonally from one letter to another, using each letter only once.

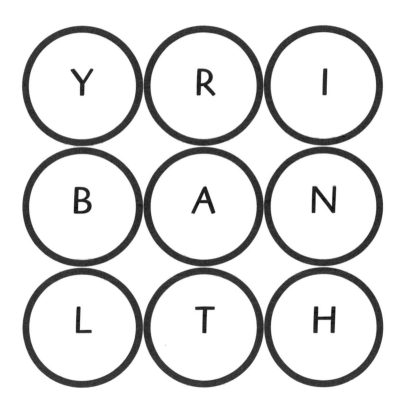

Answer:

Puzzling jars

1. Adam's dad challenges Adam and his friends, Sam and Ryan, to guess the number of marbles in a jar. Whoever is first to guess the correct answer will win a prize.

Adam guesses 136, Ryan guesses 235, and Sam guesses 105.

They're told that each of them has guessed exactly one digit correctly, and in its correct place. This is all Sam needs to guess the right answer. How many marbles are in the jar?

Answer:

2. A jar contains 25 red toffees and 50 green toffees. Next to the jar is a pile of green toffees. Alice removes toffees from the jar, following these rules:

• She takes two toffees from the jar at random.
• If at least one of them is green, she puts that one on the pile, and throws the other toffee back in the jar.
• If both toffees are red, she eats both of them, then puts a green toffee from the pile into the jar.

Each time she does this, the jar has one less toffee in it. Finally, there is just one left in the jar. Is it red, or green?

Answer:

Next-door nines

1. Nine friends are staying in the rooms at the front of this hotel, but can you puzzle out whose room is whose? Write their initials in the correct windows.

Chris's room is directly above Mandy's.
Jenny's room is not on the bottom floor.
Rob's room is directly above Harriet's.
Mandy's room is directly above Emily's and next to Alan's.
India's room is on the right, on the floor above Mandy's.
Toby's room is on the bottom floor.
Alan's room is on the left.

2. The name of the person who lives in each house is written below it. Can you work out who lives in the house that is ...

Joe	Lizzie	Sara
Louisa	Harry	Zak
Isobel	Charlie	Faye

A. ... two houses below the house that's immediately to the left of the house that's two houses above the house that's diagonally down from the house that's immediately to the left of Harry's house?

Answer:

B. ... two houses to the right of the house that's two houses below the house that's directly above the house that's immediately to the left of the house that's directly below the house that's diagonally up from Zak's house?

Answer:

Bird brain-teasers

1. These two trees both have a small flock of birds hidden amongst their leaves. If one bird from tree A flew to tree B, both the trees would have the same number of birds. But if one bird from tree B flew to tree A, tree A would have twice as many birds as tree B. Can you work out how many birds are in each tree?

A

B

2. A group of crows is flying over the fields. There are two crows in front of a crow, two crows behind a crow, and one crow in the middle. How many crows are there?

Answer:

3. If five chickens lay five eggs in five days, how many eggs will ten chickens lay in ten days?

Answer:

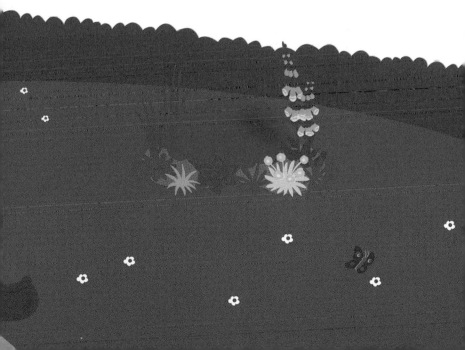

Measuring jugs

The jugs in these puzzles have no measurements on them –
you only know how much each one holds when it's full.
However, you can pour water between the jugs without
spilling any. You may need to empty or refill the jugs a few
times to solve some of the puzzles.

1. One of the jugs above can hold **ten** cups of water,
and the other can hold **four** cups. How could you use
the two jugs to measure exactly **six** cups of water?

Answer:

2. One of the jugs below can hold **four** cups of water, and the other can hold **seven** cups. How could you use the two jugs to measure exactly **five** cups of water?

Answer:

3. One of the jugs on the right can hold **five** cups of water, and the other can hold **three** cups. How could you use the two jugs to measure exactly **four** cups of water?

Answer:

Answers

1. Spot the difference:

2. Grid lines:

1.

4	3	8	2	7	6
9	5	1	9	5	1
2	7	6	4	3	8

2.

	×	×
×		×
×	×	

3. Magic bean: Thursday of the following week

4. Arctic argument:

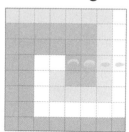

5. The magic number:
The answer is always seven.

6. Non-stop draw:

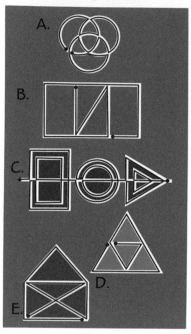

7. Making squares:

1.

2.

8. Hexagon halves:

A and D

9. Toy blocks:

1.

	5
	2
	7
	6
	1
	4
	3

2. There are six combinations:

10. Riddles:

1. Alex is *too short* to reach the twelfth button in the elevator.

2. It was daytime.

3. The hat, scarf and lumps of coal belonged to a snowman that had melted because it was a warm day.

4. There aren't any stairs.

11. Broken clock:

 (10.20)

12. Rabbit warren:

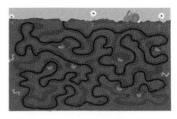

13. Word ladders:

		BEAR	TEA
		BEAT	PEA
		BELT	PET
	BUG	BELL	POT
HAND	BEG	BULL	
BAND	BEE		HEAT
BOND			HEAD
FOND		WING	HELD
FOOD	PAW	WIND	HOLD
FOOT	JAW	BIND	COLD
	JAM	BIRD	

14. Crazy cubes:

1. A, D, E   2. Eight

15. Splitting circles:

1. 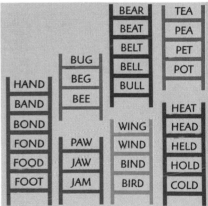   2.

16. The two mice:

Dobbin should ask either of the mice: "Which door would the other mouse tell me to go through to get to the carrots and water?" If the mouse was lying, it would say that the truthful mouse would point to the wrong door. If he asked the mouse that was telling the truth, then it would say that the lying mouse would point to the wrong door. So, whichever door the mouse points to, Dobbin should choose the other door.

17. Cog rotation:

1. He should turn it clockwise - cogs joined like this turn in the same direction:

and cogs joined like this turn the opposite way to each other:

2. A and D

18. Puzzling patterns:

1. 2.

19. Searching for shapes:

1. 23   2. 30

20. The cat in the well:

16 days – Tabby climbs out of the well before she slides down that night.

21. Counting cakes:

Five and a half cupcakes

22. Optical illusions:

1. They are the same.
2. Yellow
3. They are the same.
4. Neither, only the shadows are in different positions.

23. Flowerpots:

Answers

24. Spot the difference:

25. Dominoes:

1. A.   B.   C.

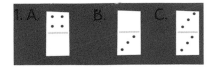

2.

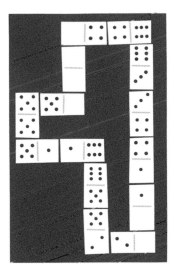

26. Troll toll:

Two bars. Every time Jake gave a troll half of his chocolate (one bar), the troll would give it back.

27. Pyramid puzzles:

1.

198
102 96
59 43 53
36 23 20 33
21 15 8 12 21
9 12 3 5 7 14

2. 37
(Five times seven is 35. Plus two makes 37.)

28. See-saws:

A. ●   B. ▲   C. ●
D. ■   E. ●

29. Shearing sheep:

30. Strange shapes:

A. I   B. P   C. I   D. P   E. I

31. Cutting hair:

As there were only two hairdressers on the island, they must cut each other's hair. Therefore, the one with the worst hair must be the better hairdresser.

Answers

32. Spiders and flies:

1. Tarantulas

2. There are two ways of doing this one:

33. Telling time:

A. (4.20) B. (9.00) C. (8.50)

34. So many triangles:

A. 35   B. 20   C. 27

35. Shape splitting:

A.   C.

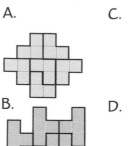

B.   D.

36. Alphabet puzzles:

1. Submarine
2. It contains every letter of the alphabet.
3. In one group, the letters only have straight lines. In the other group the letters all have curved lines in them.

37. Magician's cups:

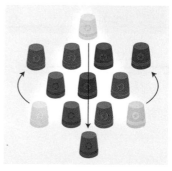

38. River crossing:

1 - Take the mouse across, leave it there.

2 - Go back alone.

3 - Take the cheese across, leave it there.

4 - Return with the mouse, leave it there.

5 - Take the cat across, leave it there.

6 - Go back alone.

7 - Take the mouse across.

This answer is also correct if you take the cat on the third crossing and take the cheese on the fifth crossing.

39. Bricks and bees:

1. Weigh any two bricks from different pairs. If they balance, then the pair of bricks that has not been weighed is the heaviest. If they don't balance, then you'll see that the heavier brick belongs to the heaviest pair.

2.

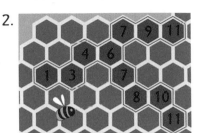

40. Tricky questions:

1. The words 'senttence' and 'misteaks' have been spelled wrongly. The third mistake is that there are only two mistakes, not three.

2. Four

3. Once, because then you don't have 39 anymore.

4. Two days

5. Thursday

6. When you give out the last orange, give it inside the bag.

41. Fencing goats:

1.   2.

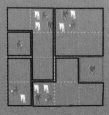

42. Star systems:

1.
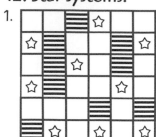

2.
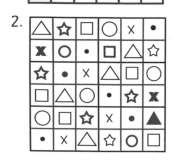

43. Joining dots:

1. 21 - there are nine small squares, then there are:

four like this: two like this:

four like this: two like this:

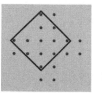

2.
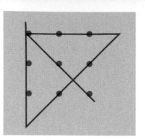

44. Crossing the bridge:

1 - Ellie (1 min.) and Josh (2 mins.) cross the bridge. (Total = 2 mins.)

2 - Josh (2 mins.) returns to the other side. (Total = 4 mins.)

3 - Isaac (5 mins.) and Mia (10 mins.) cross the bridge. (Total = 14 mins.)

4 - Ellie (1 min.) returns to the other side. (Total = 15 mins.)

5 - Ellie (1 min.) and Josh (2 mins.) cross the bridge. (Total = 17 mins.)

45. Butterfly twins:

46. Points of view:

C

47. Letters apart:

1. There are four ways of doing this:

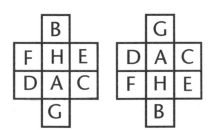

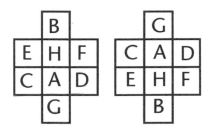

2. Labyrinth

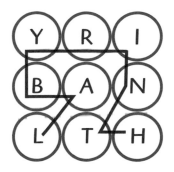

48. Puzzling jars:

1. 206

2. Red. (There is an odd number of red toffees in the jar, and they can only ever be removed in pairs, so there will be one red toffee left in the jar at the end.)

49. Next–door nines:

1.

2. A. Isobel

B. Faye

Answers

50. Bird brain-teasers:

1. There are seven birds in tree A, and five birds in tree B.

2. There are three crows, all flying in a line.

3. 20

51. Measuring jugs:

1. - Fill the ten cup jug, then pour it into the four cup jug until it is full. There will be six cups left in the ten cup jug.

2. - Fill the four cup jug, then pour it into the seven cup jug.
- Do the same again until the seven cup jug is full.

- Empty the seven cup jug.
- Pour the one cup of water left in the four cup jug into the seven cup jug.
- Fill the four cup jug again, and pour it into the seven cup jug, making a total of five cups.

3. - Fill the three cup jug, then pour it into the five cup jug.
- Do the same again until the five cup jug is full.
- Empty the five cup jug.
- Pour the one cup of water left in the three cup jug into the five cup jug.
- Fill the three cup jug again, and pour it into the five cup jug, making a total of four cups.